Gifts in a Jar create no-fuss, homemade treats your family and friends will love. Simply layer the ingredients in a 1-quart container of your choice. Be creative in selecting the perfect jar or glass canister for your gift! The most common container used for Gifts in a Jar are wide-mouth 1-quart canning jars.

- To keep mess to a minimum, shape a flexible paper plate into a funnel. Use the homemade funnel when adding each layer.

- Be sure to pack down each ingredient before adding the next.

- Lightly tap the jar on the countertop after adding ingredients like flour and powdered sugar to ensure there are no air bubbles.

- If you wish to cover your jar lid with fabric, you will need a 7″ to 8″ fabric circle. Then use a rubber band to hold the fabric in place before attaching the tag with ribbon or raffia.

- Don't forget to personalize each gift tag before attaching it to the jar.

- Make several Gifts in a Jar and include them as part of a gift basket. Personalize each basket according to the occasion or recipient. A large mixing bowl filled with Gifts in a Jar, kitchen towels, pot holders and utensils makes a great gift.

- Each gift should keep up to six months. If the mix contains nuts, it should be used within three months.

Printed in the United States of America
by G&R Publishing Co.

Published By:

507 Industrial Street
Waverly, IA 50677

ISBN-13: 978-1-56383-307-6
ISBN-10: 1-56383-307-7
Item #3012

Peach Crumb Cake Mix

¾ C. sugar
¾ C. quick oats
¾ C. brown sugar
2 C. all-purpose flour
2 tsp. baking powder
½ tsp. salt

In a 1-quart container of your choice, layer the above ingredients in order given. Pack each layer into the container before adding the next ingredient.

Securely close container and, if desired, decorate with fabric, ribbon or raffia. Cut out a gift tag with the recipient's directions from the following page. Simply personalize the tag and attach to your container.

Peach Crumb Cake

1 jar Peach Crumb Cake Mix
¾ C. butter or margarine
1 (29 oz.) can peach pie filling

Preheat oven to 350°. Empty the contents of jar into a mixing bowl, stirring to combine (if brown sugar is hard, microwave for 10 seconds). Melt butter and stir into dry ingredients to form a crumbly mixture. Press half of the crumbs into a greased 9 x 13˝ pan and top with peach pie filling. Sprinkle the remaining crumb mixture over filling. Bake for 30 to 35 minutes.

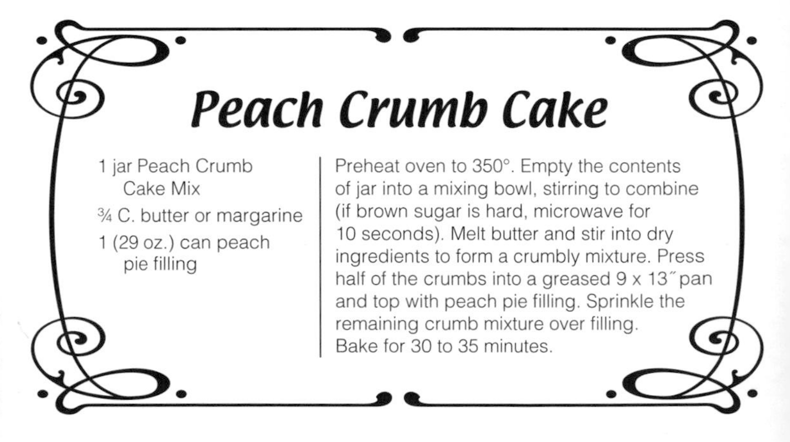

For a quality black and white reproduction, photocopy the above tag. Any of the color tags may also be photocopied for additional gifts.

Peach Crumb Cake

1 jar Peach Crumb Cake Mix
¾ C. butter or margarine
1 (29 oz.) can peach pie filling

Preheat oven to 350°. Empty the contents of jar into a mixing bowl, stirring to combine (if brown sugar is hard, microwave for 10 seconds). Melt butter and stir into dry ingredients to form a crumbly mixture. Press half of the crumbs into a greased 9 x 13″ pan and top with peach pie filling. Sprinkle the remaining crumb mixture over filling. Bake for 30 to 35 minutes.

Peach Crumb Cake

1 jar Peach Crumb Cake Mix
¾ C. butter or margarine
1 (29 oz.) can peach pie filling

Preheat oven to 350°. Empty the contents of jar into a mixing bowl, stirring to combine (if brown sugar is hard, microwave for 10 seconds). Melt butter and stir into dry ingredients to form a crumbly mixture. Press half of the crumbs into a greased 9 x 13″ pan and top with peach pie filling. Sprinkle the remaining crumb mixture over filling. Bake for 30 to 35 minutes.

Peach Crumb Cake

1 jar Peach Crumb Cake Mix
¾ C. butter or margarine
1 (29 oz.) can peach pie filling

Preheat oven to 350°. Empty the contents of jar into a mixing bowl, stirring to combine (if brown sugar is hard, microwave for 10 seconds). Melt butter and stir into dry ingredients to form a crumbly mixture. Press half of the crumbs into a greased 9 x 13″ pan and top with peach pie filling. Sprinkle the remaining crumb mixture over filling. Bake for 30 to 35 minutes.

Peach Crumb Cake

1 jar Peach Crumb Cake Mix
¾ C. butter or margarine
1 (29 oz.) can peach pie filling

Preheat oven to 350°. Empty the contents of jar into a mixing bowl, stirring to combine (if brown sugar is hard, microwave for 10 seconds). Melt butter and stir into dry ingredients to form a crumbly mixture. Press half of the crumbs into a greased 9 x 13″ pan and top with peach pie filling. Sprinkle the remaining crumb mixture over filling. Bake for 30 to 35 minutes.

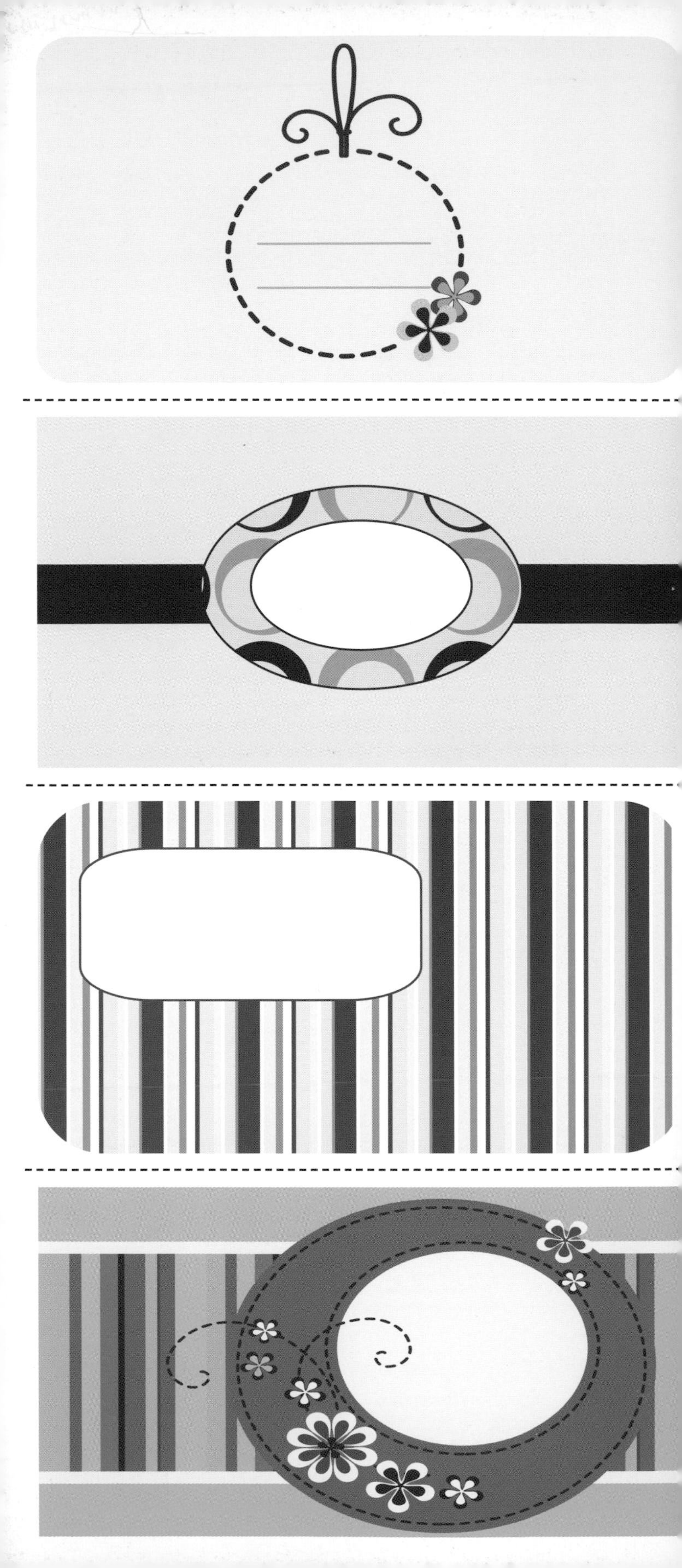

Apple Pie Wedges Mix

2⅓ C. all-purpose flour
½ C. finely chopped pecans
¾ C. dried diced apples
1 tsp. cinnamon
½ tsp. apple pie spice
⅔ C. sugar

In a 1-quart container of your choice, layer the above ingredients in order given. Pack each layer into the container before adding the next ingredient.

Securely close container and, if desired, decorate with fabric, ribbon or raffia. Cut out a gift tag with the recipient's directions from the following page. Simply personalize the tag and attach to your container.

Apple Pie Wedges

1 jar Apple Pie Wedges Mix
1 C. butter, softened
1 egg yolk
⅓ C. apple butter
½ tsp. vanilla
Frosting or cinnamon and sugar, optional

In a large bowl, pour sugar from top of jar. Add butter and beat at high speed until fluffy. Add egg yolk, apple butter and vanilla and beat at high speed for 30 seconds. Add remaining contents of jar and beat at low speed until well blended. Divide dough in half and shape each half into a 6˝ circle. Chill for 30 minutes. Remove and allow dough to warm slightly. Preheat oven to 350°. Press each circle into a greased pie pan, pressing dough halfway up sides of pan. Score dough into eight wedges and prick dough with a fork. Bake for 35 minutes. If desired, top with frosting or cinnamon and sugar.

For a quality black and white reproduction, photocopy the above tag. Any of the color tags may also be photocopied for additional gifts.

Apple Pie Wedges

- 1 jar Apple Pie Wedges Mix
- 1 C. butter, softened
- 1 egg yolk
- ⅓ C. apple butter
- ½ tsp. vanilla
- Frosting or cinnamon and sugar, optional

In a large bowl, pour sugar from top of jar. Add butter and beat at high speed until fluffy. Add egg yolk, apple butter and vanilla and beat at high speed for 30 seconds. Add remaining contents of jar and beat at low speed until well blended. Divide dough in half and shape each half into a 6″ circle. Chill for 30 minutes. Remove and allow dough to warm slightly. Preheat oven to 350°. Press each circle into a greased pie pan, pressing dough halfway up sides of pan. Score dough into eight wedges and prick dough with a fork. Bake for 35 minutes. If desired, top with frosting or cinnamon and sugar.

Apple Pie Wedges

- 1 jar Apple Pie Wedges Mix
- 1 C. butter, softened
- 1 egg yolk
- ⅓ C. apple butter
- ½ tsp. vanilla
- Frosting or cinnamon and sugar, optional

In a large bowl, pour sugar from top of jar. Add butter and beat at high speed until fluffy. Add egg yolk, apple butter and vanilla and beat at high speed for 30 seconds. Add remaining contents of jar and beat at low speed until well blended. Divide dough in half and shape each half into a 6″ circle. Chill for 30 minutes. Remove and allow dough to warm slightly. Preheat oven to 350°. Press each circle into a greased pie pan, pressing dough halfway up sides of pan. Score dough into eight wedges and prick dough with a fork. Bake for 35 minutes. If desired, top with frosting or cinnamon and sugar.

Apple Pie Wedges

- 1 jar Apple Pie Wedges Mix
- 1 C. butter, softened
- 1 egg yolk
- ⅓ C. apple butter
- ½ tsp. vanilla
- Frosting or cinnamon and sugar, optional

In a large bowl, pour sugar from top of jar. Add butter and beat at high speed until fluffy. Add egg yolk, apple butter and vanilla and beat at high speed for 30 seconds. Add remaining contents of jar and beat at low speed until well blended. Divide dough in half and shape each half into a 6″ circle. Chill for 30 minutes. Remove and allow dough to warm slightly. Preheat oven to 350°. Press each circle into a greased pie pan, pressing dough halfway up sides of pan. Score dough into eight wedges and prick dough with a fork. Bake for 35 minutes. If desired, top with frosting or cinnamon and sugar.

Apple Pie Wedges

- 1 jar Apple Pie Wedges Mix
- 1 C. butter, softened
- 1 egg yolk
- ⅓ C. apple butter
- ½ tsp. vanilla
- Frosting or cinnamon and sugar, optional

In a large bowl, pour sugar from top of jar. Add butter and beat at high speed until fluffy. Add egg yolk, apple butter and vanilla and beat at high speed for 30 seconds. Add remaining contents of jar and beat at low speed until well blended. Divide dough in half and shape each half into a 6″ circle. Chill for 30 minutes. Remove and allow dough to warm slightly. Preheat oven to 350°. Press each circle into a greased pie pan, pressing dough halfway up sides of pan. Score dough into eight wedges and prick dough with a fork. Bake for 35 minutes. If desired, top with frosting or cinnamon and sugar.

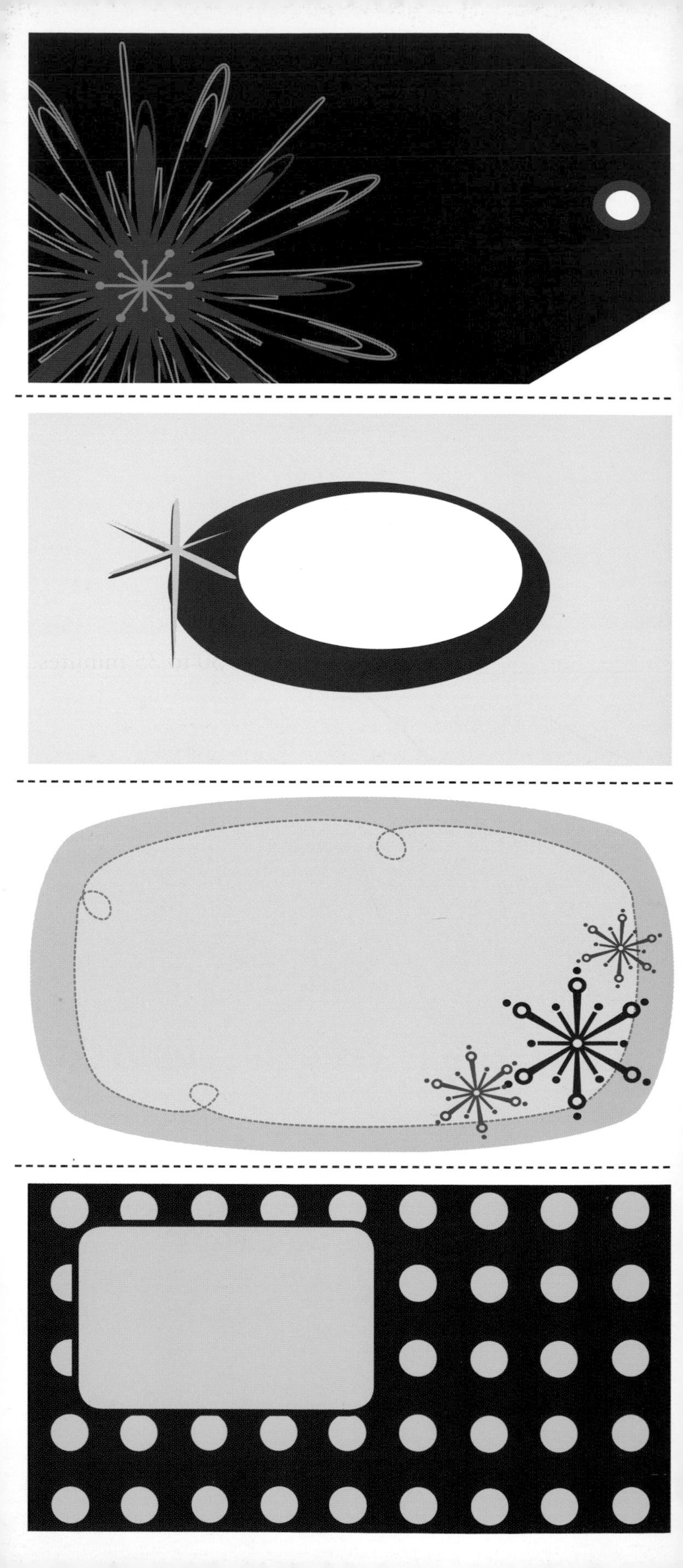

Oatmeal Chocolate Chip Bar Mix

1 C. all-purpose flour
½ C. brown sugar
½ C. sugar
1¼ C. old-fashioned oats
½ C. chopped nuts
½ tsp. baking powder
½ tsp. baking soda
½ C. chocolate chips

In a 1-quart container of your choice, layer the above ingredients in order given. Pack each layer into the container before adding the next ingredient.

Securely close container and, if desired, decorate with fabric, ribbon or raffia. Cut out a gift tag with the recipient's directions from the following page. Simply personalize the tag and attach to your container.

Oatmeal Chocolate Chip Bars

¾ C. butter or margarine, softened
4 eggs, slightly beaten
1 jar Oatmeal Chocolate Chip Bar Mix

Preheat oven to 375°. In a large bowl, cream the butter and eggs. Add the Oatmeal Chocolate Chip Bar Mix (if brown sugar is hard, microwave for 10 seconds) and stir until the mixture is well blended. Spread batter into a lightly greased 9 x 13″ pan. Bake for 20 to 25 minutes.

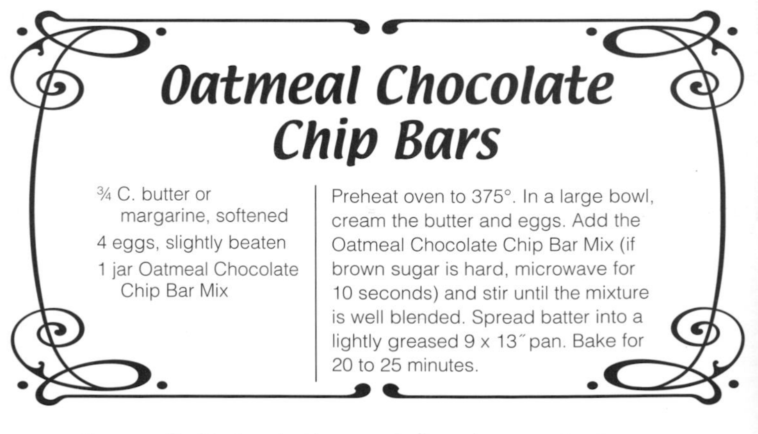

For a quality black and white reproduction, photocopy the above tag. Any of the color tags may also be photocopied for additional gifts.

Oatmeal Chocolate Chip Bars

- ¾ C. butter or margarine, softened
- 4 eggs, slightly beaten
- 1 jar Oatmeal Chocolate Chip Bar Mix

Preheat oven to 375°. In a large bowl, cream the butter and eggs. Add the Oatmeal Chocolate Chip Bar Mix (if brown sugar is hard, microwave for 10 seconds) and stir until the mixture is well blended. Spread batter into a lightly greased 9 x 13″ pan. Bake for 20 to 25 minutes.

Oatmeal Chocolate Chip Bars

- ¾ C. butter or margarine, softened
- 4 eggs, slightly beaten
- 1 jar Oatmeal Chocolate Chip Bar Mix

Preheat oven to 375°. In a large bowl, cream the butter and eggs. Add the Oatmeal Chocolate Chip Bar Mix (if brown sugar is hard, microwave for 10 seconds) and stir until the mixture is well blended. Spread batter into a lightly greased 9 x 13″ pan. Bake for 20 to 25 minutes.

Oatmeal Chocolate Chip Bars

- ¾ C. butter or margarine, softened
- 4 eggs, slightly beaten
- 1 jar Oatmeal Chocolate Chip Bar Mix

Preheat oven to 375°. In a large bowl, cream the butter and eggs. Add the Oatmeal Chocolate Chip Bar Mix (if brown sugar is hard, microwave for 10 seconds) and stir until the mixture is well blended. Spread batter into a lightly greased 9 x 13″ pan. Bake for 20 to 25 minutes.

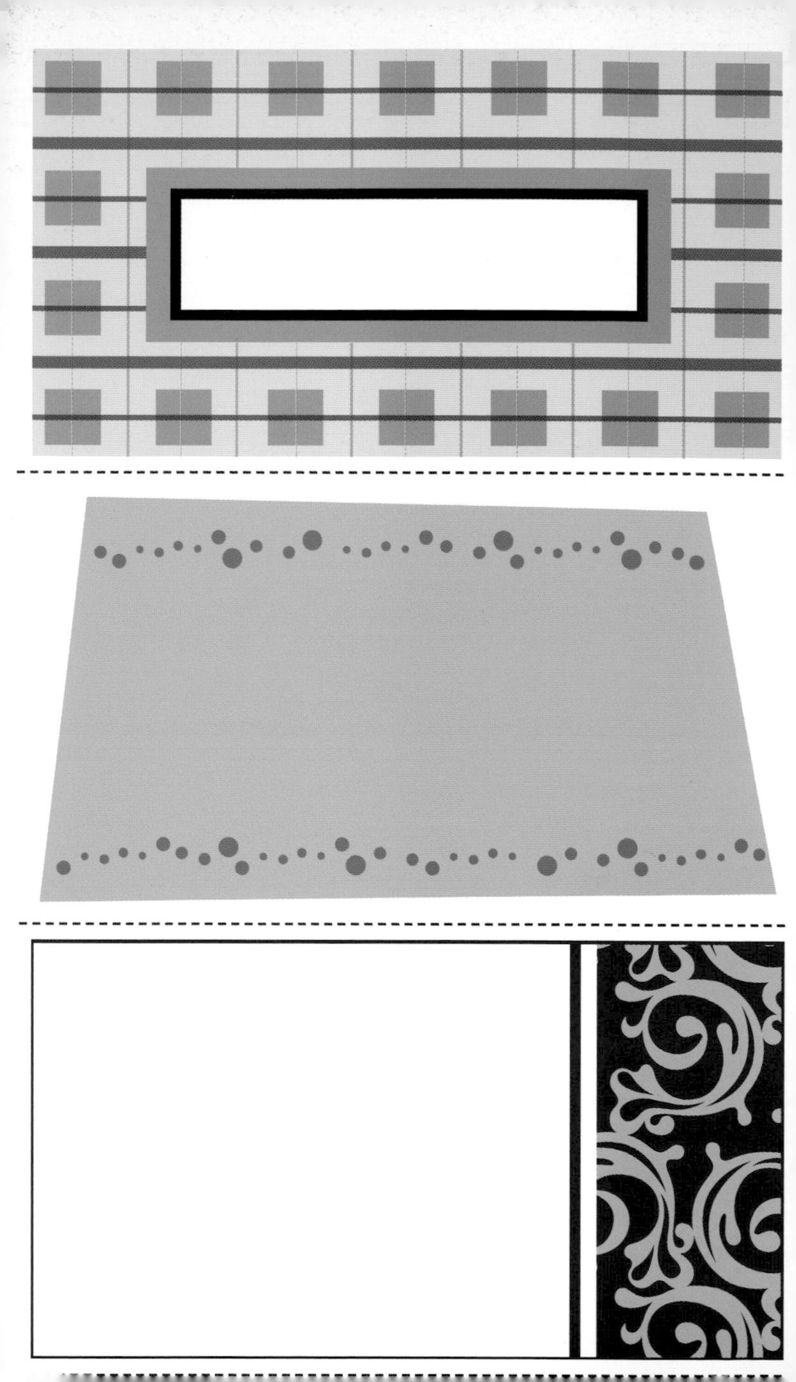

Double Chocolate Nut Cake Mix

⅓ C. cocoa powder
½ C. sugar
¾ C. chocolate chips
½ C. chopped walnuts or pecans
½ C. brown sugar
1½ tsp. baking soda
½ tsp. salt
1⅔ C. all-purpose flour

In a 1-quart container of your choice, layer the above ingredients in order given. After adding the unsweetened cocoa, but before adding the flour, clean the inside of the jar with a paper towel. Pack each layer into the container before adding the next ingredient.

Securely close container and, if desired, decorate with fabric, ribbon or raffia. Cut out a gift tag with the recipient's directions from the following page. Simply personalize the tag and attach to your container.

Double Chocolate Nut Cake

1 jar Double Chocolate Nut Cake Mix
1 C. water
⅓ C. vegetable oil
1 tsp. vinegar
1 tsp. vanilla

Preheat oven to 350°. In a large bowl, add contents of jar (if brown sugar is hard, microwave for 10 seconds). Add water, vegetable oil, vinegar and vanilla and mix until well combined. Pour batter into a lightly greased and floured 8 x 8″ pan. Bake for 40 to 45 minutes.

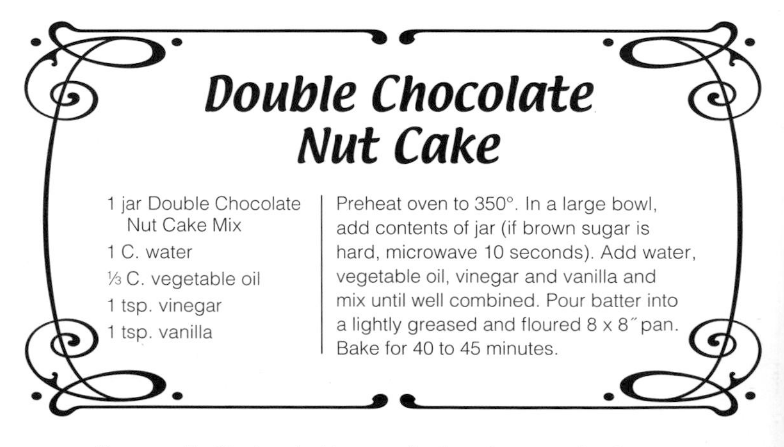

For a quality black and white reproduction, photocopy the above tag. Any of the color tags may also be photocopied for additional gifts.

Double Chocolate Nut Cake

- 1 jar Double Chocolate Nut Cake Mix
- 1 C. water
- ⅓ C. vegetable oil
- 1 tsp. vinegar
- 1 tsp. vanilla

Preheat oven to 350°. In a large bowl, add contents of jar (if brown sugar is hard, microwave 10 seconds). Add water, vegetable oil, vinegar and vanilla and mix until well combined. Pour batter into a lightly greased and floured 8 x 8″ pan. Bake for 40 to 45 minutes.

Double Chocolate Nut Cake

- 1 jar Double Chocolate Nut Cake Mix
- 1 C. water
- ⅓ C. vegetable oil
- 1 tsp. vinegar
- 1 tsp. vanilla

Preheat oven to 350°. In a large bowl, add contents of jar (if brown sugar is hard, microwave 10 seconds). Add water, vegetable oil, vinegar and vanilla and mix until well combined. Pour batter into a lightly greased and floured 8 x 8″ pan. Bake for 40 to 45 minutes.

Double Chocolate Nut Cake

- 1 jar Double Chocolate Nut Cake Mix
- 1 C. water
- ⅓ C. vegetable oil
- 1 tsp. vinegar
- 1 tsp. vanilla

Preheat oven to 350°. In a large bowl, add contents of jar (if brown sugar is hard, microwave 10 seconds). Add water, vegetable oil, vinegar and vanilla and mix until well combined. Pour batter into a lightly greased and floured 8 x 8″ pan. Bake for 40 to 45 minutes.

Double Chocolate Nut Cake

- 1 jar Double Chocolate Nut Cake Mix
- 1 C. water
- ⅓ C. vegetable oil
- 1 tsp. vinegar
- 1 tsp. vanilla

Preheat oven to 350°. In a large bowl, add contents of jar (if brown sugar is hard, microwave 10 seconds). Add water, vegetable oil, vinegar and vanilla and mix until well combined. Pour batter into a lightly greased and floured 8 x 8″ pan. Bake for 40 to 45 minutes.

Almond Buttercrunch Candy Mix

¼ C. milk chocolate chips
½ C. blanched slivered almonds
2 C. milk chocolate chips
½ C. blanched slivered almonds

In a plastic bag place:
1 C. brown sugar

In a 1-quart container of your choice, layer the above ingredients in order given. Pack each layer into the container before adding the next ingredient. Place the brown sugar-filled bag in the container on top of other ingredients.

Securely close container and, if desired, decorate with fabric, ribbon or raffia. Cut out a gift tag with the recipient's directions from the following page. Simply personalize the tag and attach to your container.

Almond Buttercrunch Candy

1 jar Almond Buttercrunch Candy Mix
1 C. butter
2 Hershey's chocolate bars, broken

Preheat oven to 200°. Remove plastic bag from jar and set aside. Pour ½ cup almonds from top of jar and set aside. Pour remaining contents of jar into a greased 9 x 13″ pan. Place in oven until chocolate melts. Remove from oven and spread mixture over bottom of pan. In a heavy saucepan over medium-high heat, melt butter and brown sugar from bag. Heat, stirring constantly, until mixture reaches 300°. Pour mixture evenly over ingredients in pan. Sprinkle reserved almonds and broken chocolate bars over sugar mixture. Let cool before cutting into pieces.

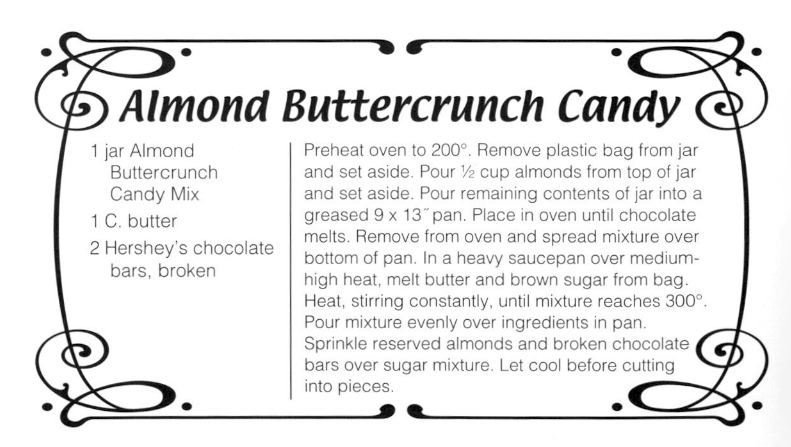

Almond Buttercrunch Candy

1 jar Almond Buttercrunch Candy Mix
1 C. butter
2 Hershey's chocolate bars, broken

Preheat oven to 200°. Remove plastic bag from jar and set aside. Pour ½ cup almonds from top of jar and set aside. Pour remaining contents of jar into a greased 9 x 13″ pan. Place in oven until chocolate melts. Remove from oven and spread mixture over bottom of pan. In a heavy saucepan over medium-high heat, melt butter and brown sugar from bag. Heat, stirring constantly, until mixture reaches 300°. Pour mixture evenly over ingredients in pan. Sprinkle reserved almonds and broken chocolate bars over sugar mixture. Let cool before cutting into pieces.

For a quality black and white reproduction, photocopy the above tag. Any of the color tags may also be photocopied for additional gifts.

Almond Buttercrunch Candy

- 1 jar Almond Buttercrunch Candy Mix
- 1 C. butter
- 2 Hershey's chocolate bars, broken

Preheat oven to 200°. Remove plastic bag from jar and set aside. Pour ½ cup almonds from top of jar and set aside. Pour remaining contents of jar into a greased 9 x 13″ pan. Place in oven until chocolate melts. Remove from oven and spread mixture over bottom of pan. In a heavy saucepan over medium-high heat, melt butter and brown sugar from bag. Heat, stirring constantly, until mixture reaches 300°. Pour mixture evenly over ingredients in pan. Sprinkle reserved almonds and broken chocolate bars over sugar mixture. Let cool before cutting into pieces.

Almond Buttercrunch Candy

- 1 jar Almond Butter crunch Candy Mix
- 1 C. butter
- 2 Hershey's chocolate bars, broken

Preheat oven to 200°. Remove plastic bag from jar and set aside. Pour ½ cup almonds from top of jar and set aside. Pour remaining contents of jar into a greased 9 x 13″ pan. Place in oven until chocolate melts. Remove from oven and spread mixture over bottom of pan. In a heavy saucepan over medium-high heat, melt butter and brown sugar from bag. Heat, stirring constantly, until mixture reaches 300°. Pour mixture evenly over ingredients in pan. Sprinkle reserved almonds and broken chocolate bars over sugar mixture. Let cool before cutting into pieces.

Almond Buttercrunch Candy

- 1 jar Almond Buttercrunch Candy Mix
- 1 C. butter
- 2 Hershey's chocolate bars, broken

Preheat oven to 200°. Remove plastic bag from jar and set aside. Pour ½ cup almonds from top of jar and set aside. Pour remaining contents of jar into a greased 9 x 13″ pan. Place in oven until chocolate melts. Remove from oven and spread mixture over bottom of pan. In a heavy saucepan over medium-high heat, melt butter and brown sugar from bag. Heat, stirring constantly, until mixture reaches 300°. Pour mixture evenly over ingredients in pan. Sprinkle reserved almonds and broken chocolate bars over sugar mixture. Let cool before cutting into pieces.

Almond Buttercrunch Candy

- 1 jar Almond Buttercrunch Candy Mix
- 1 C. butter
- 2 Hershey's chocolate bars, broken

Preheat oven to 200°. Remove plastic bag from jar and set aside. Pour ½ cup almonds from top of jar and set aside. Pour remaining contents of jar into a greased 9 x 13″ pan. Place in oven until chocolate melts. Remove from oven and spread mixture over bottom of pan. In a heavy saucepan over medium-high heat, melt butter and brown sugar from bag. Heat, stirring constantly, until mixture reaches 300°. Pour mixture evenly over ingredients in pan. Sprinkle reserved almonds and broken chocolate bars over sugar mixture. Let cool before cutting into pieces.

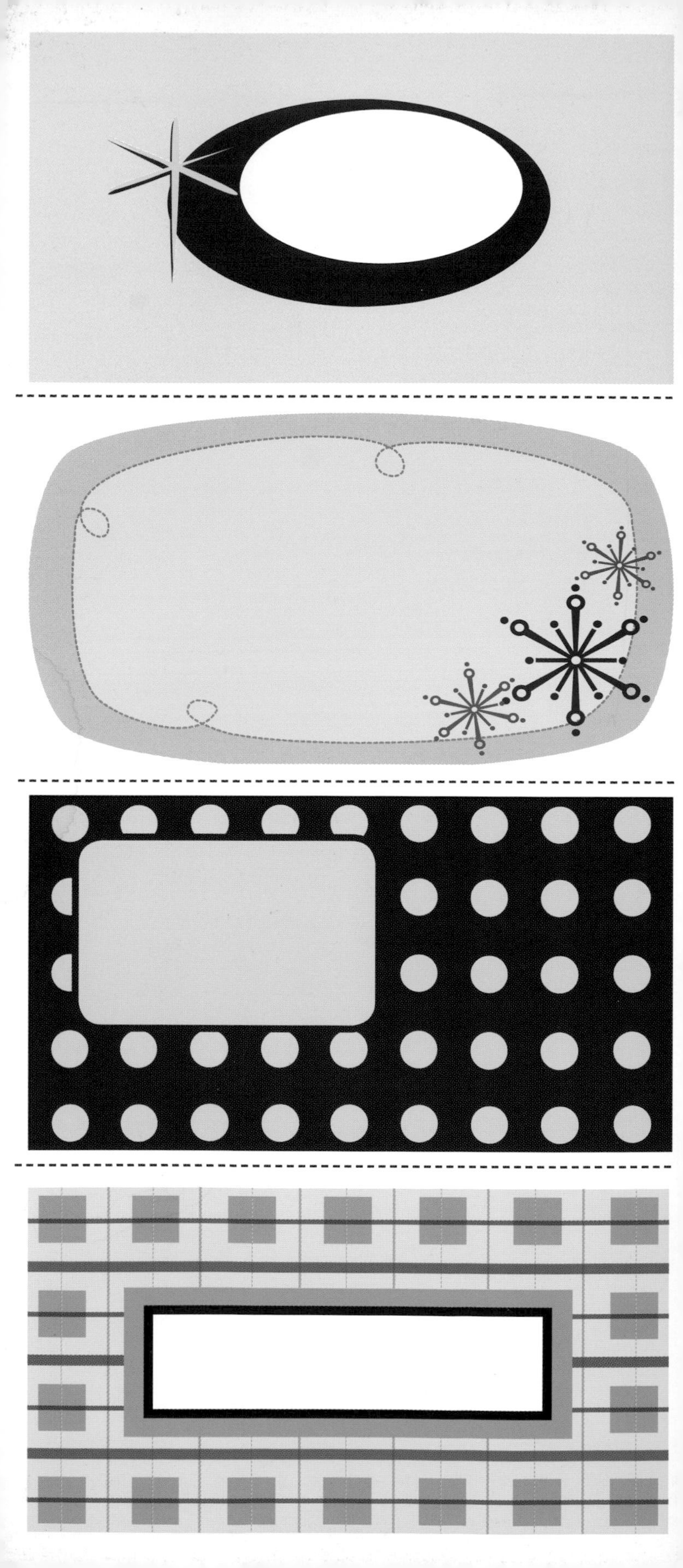

Deluxe Chocolate Chunk Cookie Mix

½ C. finely chopped walnuts
1 C. semi-sweet chocolate chunks
1 tsp. baking soda
¼ tsp. salt
½ tsp. baking powder
1½ C. all-purpose flour
⅔ C. brown sugar
⅔ C. sugar

In a 1-quart container of your choice, layer the above ingredients in order given. Pack each layer into the container before adding the next ingredient.

Securely close container and, if desired, decorate with fabric, ribbon or raffia. Cut out a gift tag with the recipient's directions from the following page. Simply personalize the tag and attach to your container.

Deluxe Chocolate Chunk Cookies

1 jar Deluxe Chocolate Chunk Cookie Mix
⅓ C. shortening
⅓ C. margarine, softened
1 egg
1 tsp. vanilla

Preheat oven to 375°. In a large mixing bowl, pour sugar and brown sugar from top of jar (if brown sugar is hard, microwave for 10 seconds). Add shortening and margarine and mix at high speed until lightened in texture. Add egg and vanilla and beat at high speed for 1 to 2 minutes. Add remaining contents of jar and beat at low speed until combined. Drop dough by teaspoonfuls onto a lightly greased baking sheet. Bake for 8 to 10 minutes.

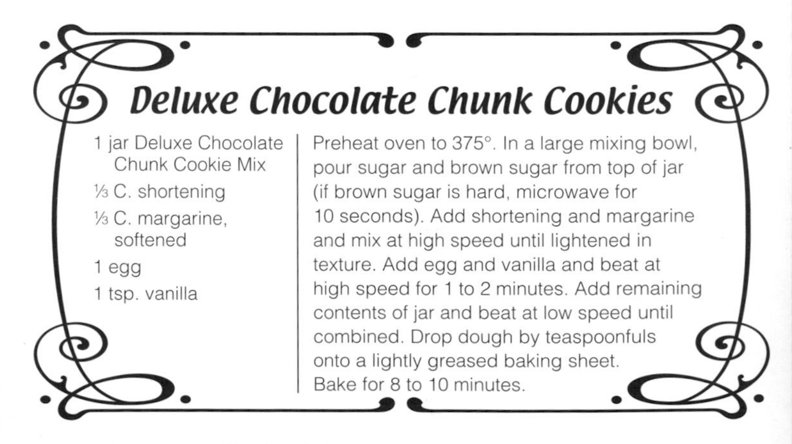

For a quality black and white reproduction, photocopy the above tag. Any of the color tags may also be photocopied for additional gifts.

Deluxe Chocolate Chunk Cookies

1 jar Deluxe Chocolate Chunk Cookie Mix
⅓ C. shortening
⅓ C. margarine, softened
1 egg
1 tsp. vanilla

Preheat oven to 375°. In a large mixing bowl, pour sugar and brown sugar from top of jar (if brown sugar is hard, microwave 10 seconds). Add shortening and margarine and mix at high speed until lightened in texture. Add egg and vanilla and beat at high speed for 1 to 2 minutes. Add remaining contents of jar and beat at low speed until combined. Drop dough by teaspoonfuls onto a lightly greased baking sheet. Bake for 8 to 10 minutes.

Deluxe Chocolate Chunk Cookies

1 jar Deluxe Chocolate Chunk Cookie Mix
⅓ C. shortening
⅓ C. margarine, softened
1 egg
1 tsp. vanilla

Preheat oven to 375°. In a large mixing bowl, pour sugar and brown sugar from top of jar (if brown sugar is hard, microwave 10 seconds). Add shortening and margarine and mix at high speed until lightened in texture. Add egg and vanilla and beat at high speed for 1 to 2 minutes. Add remaining contents of jar and beat at low speed until combined. Drop dough by teaspoonfuls onto a lightly greased baking sheet. Bake for 8 to 10 minutes.

Deluxe Chocolate Chunk Cookies

1 jar Deluxe Chocolate Chunk Cookie Mix
⅓ C. shortening
⅓ C. margarine, softened
1 egg
1 tsp. vanilla

Preheat oven to 375°. In a large mixing bowl, pour sugar and brown sugar from top of jar (if brown sugar is hard, microwave for 10 seconds). Add shortening and margarine and mix at high speed until lightened in texture. Add egg and vanilla and beat at high speed for 1 to 2 minutes. Add remaining contents of jar and beat at low speed until combined. Drop dough by teaspoonfuls onto a lightly greased baking sheet. Bake for 8 to 10 minutes.

Peanut-Cashew Cluster Mix

1 C. peanut butter chips
1 C. cashews
1¼ C. chocolate chips
1 C. dry roasted peanuts

In a 1-quart container of your choice, layer the above ingredients in order given. Pack each layer into the container before adding the next ingredient.

Securely close container and, if desired, decorate with fabric, ribbon or raffia. Cut out a gift tag with the recipient's directions from the following page. Simply personalize the tag and attach to your container.

Peanut-Cashew Clusters

1 jar Peanut-Cashew Cluster Mix
3 T. butter
1½ T. half & half

In the top of a double boiler, add contents of jar. Add butter and half & half and cook over boiling water, stirring constantly, until peanut butter chips and chocolate chips are melted. Let cool slightly and drop by teaspoonfuls onto waxed paper. Chill in refrigerator until hardened.

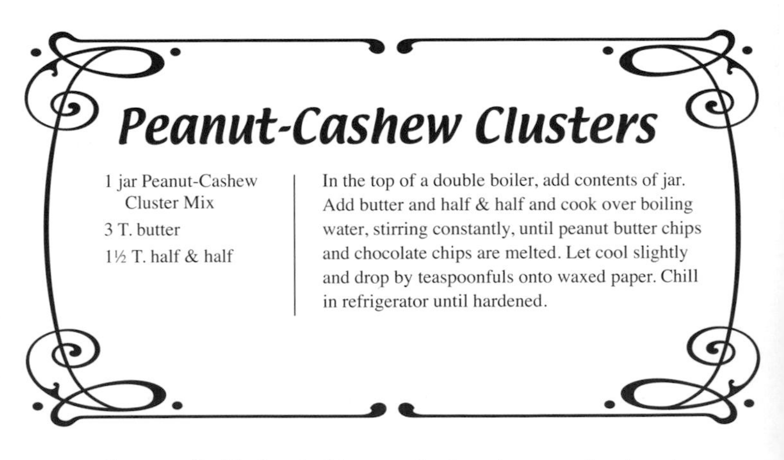

For a quality black and white reproduction, photocopy the above tag. Any of the color tags may also be photocopied for additional gifts.

Peanut-Cashew Clusters

1 jar Peanut-Cashew Cluster Mix
3 T. butter
1½ T. half & half

In the top of a double boiler, add contents of jar. Add butter and half & half and cook over boiling water, stirring constantly, until peanut butter chips and chocolate chips are melted. Let cool slightly and drop by teaspoonfuls onto waxed paper. Chill in refrigerator until hardened.

Peanut-Cashew Clusters

1 jar Peanut-Cashew Cluster Mix
3 T. butter
1½ T. half & half

In the top of a double boiler, add contents of jar. Add butter and half & half and cook over boiling water, stirring constantly, until peanut butter chips and chocolate chips are melted. Let cool slightly and drop by teaspoonfuls onto waxed paper. Chill in refrigerator until hardened.

Peanut-Cashew Clusters

1 jar Peanut-Cashew Cluster Mix
3 T. butter
1½ T. half & half

In the top of a double boiler, add contents of jar. Add butter and half & half and cook over boiling water, stirring constantly, until peanut butter chips and chocolate chips are melted. Let cool slightly and drop by teaspoonfuls onto waxed paper. Chill in refrigerator until hardened.

Peanut-Cashew Clusters

1 jar Peanut-Cashew Cluster Mix
3 T. butter
1½ T. half & half

In the top of a double boiler, add contents of jar. Add butter and half & half and cook over boiling water, stirring constantly, until peanut butter chips and chocolate chips are melted. Let cool slightly and drop by teaspoonfuls onto waxed paper. Chill in refrigerator until hardened.

Devil's Food Cake Mix

½ C. sugar
½ C. cocoa powder
¾ C. sugar
¾ C. mini chocolate chips
1¾ C. all-purpose flour
1 tsp. baking soda
¾ tsp. baking powder
¾ tsp. salt

In a 1-quart container of your choice, layer the above ingredients in order given. After adding the unsweetened cocoa, but before adding the flour, clean the inside of the jar with a paper towel. Pack each layer into the container before adding the next ingredient.

Securely close container and, if desired, decorate with fabric, ribbon or raffia. Cut out a gift tag with the recipient's directions from the following page. Simply personalize the tag and attach to your container.

Devil's Food Cake

1 jar Devil's Food Cake Mix
¾ C. shortening
1¼ C. milk, divided
1 tsp. vanilla
2 eggs

Preheat oven to 350°. In a large mixing bowl, empty contents of jar. Add shortening and mix at medium speed for 1 to 2 minutes, until well mixed. Add ¾ cup milk and vanilla and mix at medium speed for 1 to 2 minutes, scraping sides of bowl occasionally. Add eggs and remaining ½ cup milk and beat for 1 additional minute. Pour batter into a lightly greased and floured 9 x 13″ pan. Bake for 35 to 40 minutes.

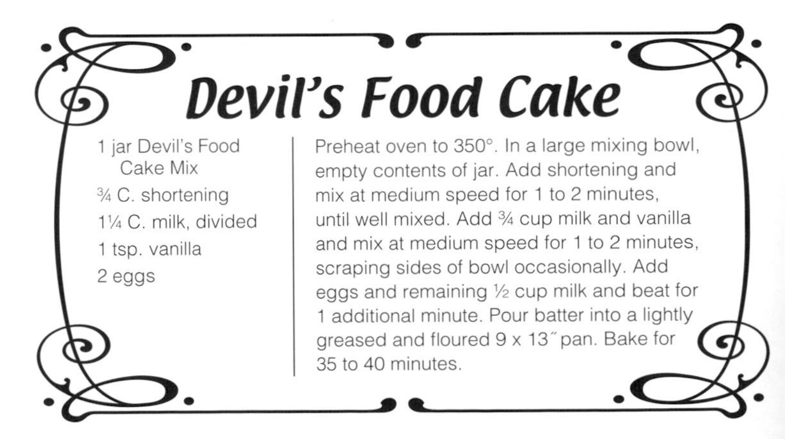

For a quality black and white reproduction, photocopy the above tag. Any of the color tags may also be photocopied for additional gifts.

Devil's Food Cake

- 1 jar Devil's Food Cake Mix
- ¾ C. shortening
- 1¼ C. milk, divided
- 1 tsp. vanilla
- 2 eggs

Preheat oven to 350°. In a large mixing bowl, empty contents of jar. Add shortening and mix at medium speed for 1 to 2 minutes, until well mixed. Add ¾ cup milk and vanilla and mix at medium speed for 1 to 2 minutes, scraping sides of bowl occasionally. Add eggs and remaining ½ cup milk and beat for 1 additional minute. Pour batter into a lightly greased and floured 9 x 13″ pan. Bake for 35 to 40 minutes.

Devil's Food Cake

- 1 jar Devil's Food Cake Mix
- ¾ C. shortening
- 1¼ C. milk, divided
- 1 tsp. vanilla
- 2 eggs

Preheat oven to 350°. In a large mixing bowl, empty contents of jar. Add shortening and mix at medium speed for 1 to 2 minutes, until well mixed. Add ¾ cup milk and vanilla and mix at medium speed for 1 to 2 minutes, scraping sides of bowl occasionally. Add eggs and remaining ½ cup milk and beat for 1 additional minute. Pour batter into a lightly greased and floured 9 x 13″ pan. Bake for 35 to 40 minutes.

Devil's Food Cake

- 1 jar Devil's Food Cake Mix
- ¾ C. shortening
- 1¼ C. milk, divided
- 1 tsp. vanilla
- 2 eggs

Preheat oven to 350°. In a large mixing bowl, empty contents of jar. Add shortening and mix at medium speed for 1 to 2 minutes, until well mixed. Add ¾ cup milk and vanilla and mix at medium speed for 1 to 2 minutes, scraping sides of bowl occasionally. Add eggs and remaining ½ cup milk and beat for 1 additional minute. Pour batter into a lightly greased and floured 9 x 13″ pan. Bake for 35 to 40 minutes.

Devil's Food Cake

- 1 jar Devil's Food Cake Mix
- ¾ C. shortening
- 1¼ C. milk, divided
- 1 tsp. vanilla
- 2 eggs

Preheat oven to 350°. In a large mixing bowl, empty contents of jar. Add shortening and mix at medium speed for 1 to 2 minutes, until well mixed. Add ¾ cup milk and vanilla and mix at medium speed for 1 to 2 minutes, scraping sides of bowl occasionally. Add eggs and remaining ½ cup milk and beat for 1 additional minute. Pour batter into a lightly greased and floured 9 x 13″ pan. Bake for 35 to 40 minutes.

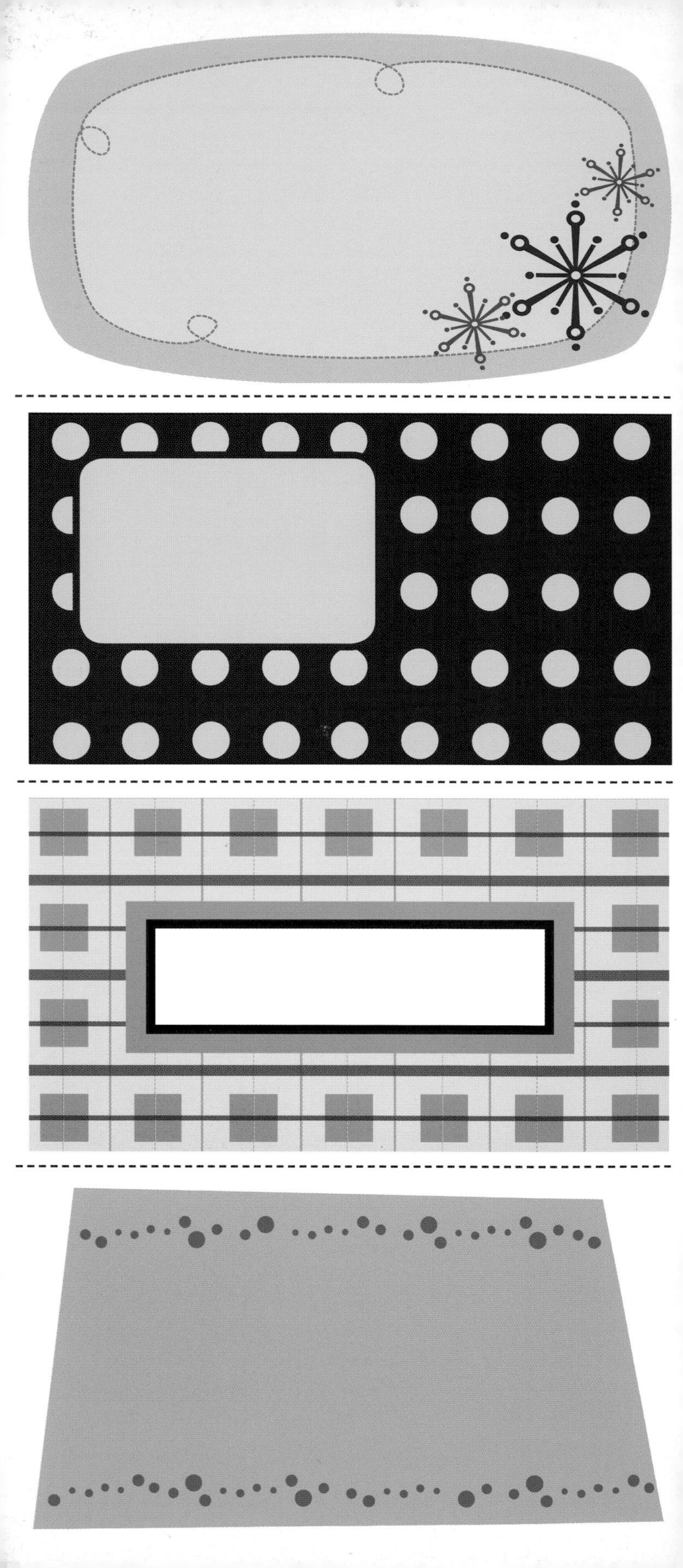

Oatmeal Coconut Crispies Mix

¾ C. shredded coconut
1 C. quick oats
1½ C. all-purpose flour
¾ tsp. baking soda
½ tsp. salt
½ C. brown sugar
½ C. sugar

In a 1-quart container of your choice, layer the above ingredients in order given. Pack each layer into the container before adding the next ingredient.

Securely close container and, if desired, decorate with fabric, ribbon or raffia. Cut out a gift tag with the recipient's directions from the following page. Simply personalize the tag and attach to your container.

Oatmeal Coconut Crispies

1 jar Oatmeal Coconut Crispies Mix
⅔ C. shortening
1 egg
1 tsp. vanilla

Preheat oven to 375°. In a large mixing bowl, pour sugar and brown sugar from top of jar (if brown sugar is hard, microwave 10 seconds). Add shortening and mix at high speed until lightened in texture. Add egg and vanilla and beat at high speed for 1 to 2 minutes. Add remaining ingredients from jar and beat at low speed just until combined. Drop dough by teaspoonfuls onto a lightly greased baking sheet. Bake for 8 to 10 minutes.

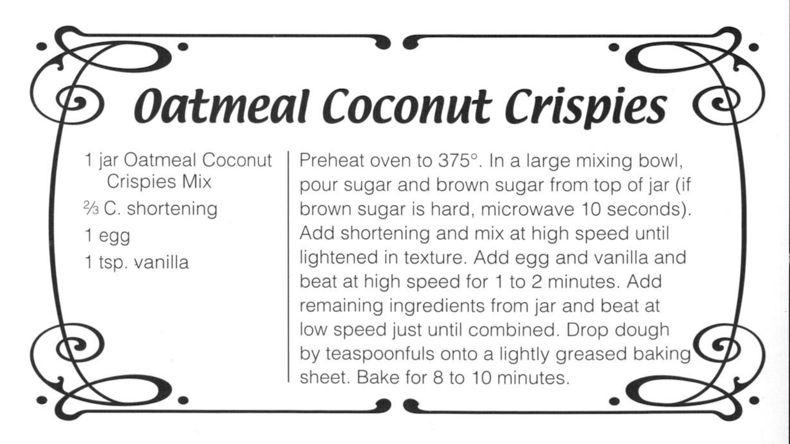
Oatmeal Coconut Crispies

1 jar Oatmeal Coconut Crispies Mix
⅔ C. shortening
1 egg
1 tsp. vanilla

Preheat oven to 375°. In a large mixing bowl, pour sugar and brown sugar from top of jar (if brown sugar is hard, microwave 10 seconds). Add shortening and mix at high speed until lightened in texture. Add egg and vanilla and beat at high speed for 1 to 2 minutes. Add remaining ingredients from jar and beat at low speed just until combined. Drop dough by teaspoonfuls onto a lightly greased baking sheet. Bake for 8 to 10 minutes.

For a quality black and white reproduction, photocopy the above tag. Any of the color tags may also be photocopied for additional gifts.

Oatmeal Coconut Crispies

- 1 jar Oatmeal Coconut Crispies Mix
- ⅔ C. shortening
- 1 egg
- 1 tsp. vanilla

Preheat oven to 375°. In a large mixing bowl, pour sugar and brown sugar from top of jar (if brown sugar is hard, microwave for 10 seconds). Add shortening and mix at high speed until lightened in texture. Add egg and vanilla and beat at high speed for 1 to 2 minutes. Add remaining ingredients from jar and beat at low speed just until combined. Drop dough by teaspoonfuls onto a lightly greased baking sheet. Bake for 8 to 10 minutes.

Oatmeal Coconut Crispies

- 1 jar Oatmeal Coconut Crispies Mix
- ⅔ C. shortening
- 1 egg
- 1 tsp. vanilla

Preheat oven to 375°. In a large mixing bowl, pour sugar and brown sugar from top of jar (if brown sugar is hard, microwave 10 seconds). Add shortening and mix at high speed until lightened in texture. Add egg and vanilla and beat at high speed for 1 to 2 minutes. Add remaining ingredients from jar and beat at low speed just until combined. Drop dough by teaspoonfuls onto a lightly greased baking sheet. Bake for 8 to 10 minutes.

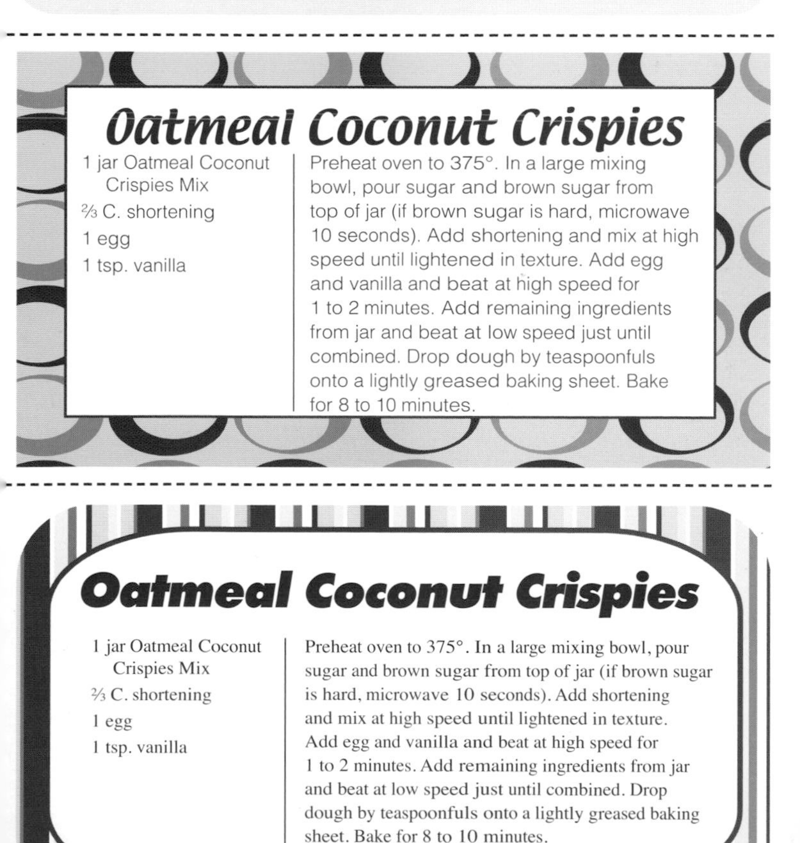

Oatmeal Coconut Crispies

- 1 jar Oatmeal Coconut Crispies Mix
- ⅔ C. shortening
- 1 egg
- 1 tsp. vanilla

Preheat oven to 375°. In a large mixing bowl, pour sugar and brown sugar from top of jar (if brown sugar is hard, microwave 10 seconds). Add shortening and mix at high speed until lightened in texture. Add egg and vanilla and beat at high speed for 1 to 2 minutes. Add remaining ingredients from jar and beat at low speed just until combined. Drop dough by teaspoonfuls onto a lightly greased baking sheet. Bake for 8 to 10 minutes.

Oatmeal Coconut Crispies

- 1 jar Oatmeal Coconut Crispies Mix
- ⅔ C. shortening
- 1 egg
- 1 tsp. vanilla

Preheat oven to 375°. In a large mixing bowl, pour sugar and brown sugar from top of jar (if brown sugar is hard, microwave 10 seconds). Add shortening and mix at high speed until lightened in texture. Add egg and vanilla and beat at high speed for 1 to 2 minutes. Add remaining ingredients from jar and beat at low speed just until combined. Drop dough by teaspoonfuls onto a lightly greased baking sheet. Bake for 8 to 10 minutes.

Caramel Rum Fondue Mix

20 pieces caramel candies, unwrapped
1 C. mini marshmallows
½ C. brown sugar
½ C. white sugar
20 pieces caramel candies, unwrapped
1 C. mini marshmallows

In a 1-quart container of your choice, layer the above ingredients in order given. Pack each layer into the container before adding the next ingredient.

Securely close container and, if desired, decorate with fabric, ribbon or raffia. Cut out a gift tag with the recipient's directions from the following page. Simply personalize the tag and attach to your container.

Caramel Rum Fondue

1 jar Caramel Run Fondue Mix
¾ C. whipping cream or whole milk
1 T. rum or ½ tsp. rum flavoring

Empty the contents of jar into slow cooker, stirring to mix. Turn slow cooker on high heat and add whipping cream or milk. Be sure to stir fondue every 10 minutes. Once caramels are melted, add rum or rum flavoring. Continue stirring every 10 minutes. This makes a great dessert fondue for fruits, pound cake, vanilla wafers and other cookies.

For a quality black and white reproduction, photocopy the above tag. Any of the color tags may also be photocopied for additional gifts.

Caramel Rum Fondue

- 1 jar Caramel Rum Fondue Mix
- ¾ C. whipping cream or whole milk
- 1 T. rum or ½ tsp. rum flavoring

Empty the contents of jar into slow cooker, stirring to mix. Turn slow cooker on high heat and add whipping cream or milk. Be sure to stir fondue every 10 minutes. Once caramels are melted, add rum or rum flavoring. Continue stirring every 10 minutes. This makes a great dessert fondue for fruits, pound cake, vanilla wafers and other cookies.

Caramel Rum Fondue

- 1 jar Caramel Rum Fondue Mix
- ¾ C. whipping cream or whole milk
- 1 T. rum or ½ tsp. rum flavoring

Empty the contents of jar into slow cooker, stirring to mix. Turn slow cooker on high heat and add whipping cream or milk. Be sure to stir fondue every 10 minutes. Once caramels are melted, add rum or rum lavoring. Continue stirring every 10 minutes. This makes a great dessert fondue for fruits, pound cake, vanilla wafers and other cookies.

Caramel Rum Fondue

- 1 jar Caramel Rum Fondue Mix
- ¾ C. whipping cream or whole milk
- 1 T. rum or ½ tsp. rum flavoring

Empty the contents of jar into slow cooker, stirring to mix. Turn slow cooker on high heat and add whipping cream or milk. Be sure to stir fondue every 10 minutes. Once caramels are melted, add rum or rum flavoring. Continue stirring every 10 minutes. This makes a great dessert fondue for fruits, pound cake, vanilla wafers and other cookies.

Caramel Rum Fondue

- 1 jar Caramel Run Fondue Mix
- ¾ C. whipping cream or whole milk
- 1 T. rum or ½ tsp. rum flavoring

Empty the contents of jar into slow cooker, stirring to mix. Turn slow cooker on high heat and add whipping cream or milk. Be sure to stir fondue every 10 minutes. Once caramels are melted, add rum or rum flavoring. Continue stirring every 10 minutes. This makes a great dessert fondue for fruits, pound cake, vanilla wafers and other cookies.

White Chocolate & Cranberry Cookie Mix

1 C. white baking chips
⅔ C. dried cranberries
1 tsp. baking soda
½ tsp. baking powder
¼ tsp. salt
1⅔ C. all-purpose flour
⅔ C. brown sugar
⅓ C. sugar

In a 1-quart container of your choice, layer the above ingredients in order given. Pack each layer into the container before adding the next ingredient.

Securely close container and, if desired, decorate with fabric, ribbon or raffia. Cut out a gift tag with the recipient's directions from the following page. Simply personalize the tag and attach to your container.

White Chocolate & Cranberry Cookies

1 jar White Chocolate & Cranberry Cookie Mix
¾ C. butter, softened
1 egg

Preheat oven to 375°. In a large mixing bowl, pour sugar and brown sugar from top of jar (if brown sugar is hard, microwave 10 seconds). Add butter and mix at high speed until lightened in texture. Add egg and beat at high speed for 1 to 2 minutes. Add remaining ingredients from jar and beat at low speed until well combined. Drop dough by teaspoonfuls onto a lightly greased baking sheet. Bake for 8 to 10 minutes.

For a quality black and white reproduction, photocopy the above tag. Any of the color tags may also be photocopied for additional gifts.

White Chocolate & Cranberry Cookies

1 jar White Chocolate & Cranberry Cookie Mix

¾ C. butter, softened

1 egg

Preheat oven to 375°. In a large mixing bowl, pour sugar and brown sugar from top of jar (if brown sugar is hard, microwave 10 seconds). Add butter and mix at high speed until lightened in texture. Add egg and beat at high speed for 1 to 2 minutes. Add remaining ingredients from jar and beat at low speed until well combined. Drop dough by teaspoonfuls onto a lightly greased baking sheet. Bake for 8 to 10 minutes.

White Chocolate & Cranberry Cookies

1 jar White Chocolate & Cranberry Cookie Mix

¾ C. butter, softened

1 egg

Preheat oven to 375°. In a large mixing bowl, pour sugar and brown sugar from top of jar (if brown sugar is hard, microwave 10 seconds). Add butter and mix at high speed until lightened in texture. Add egg and beat at high speed for 1 to 2 minutes. Add remaining ingredients from jar and beat at low speed until well combined. Drop dough by teaspoonfuls onto a lightly greased baking sheet. Bake for 8 to 10 minutes.

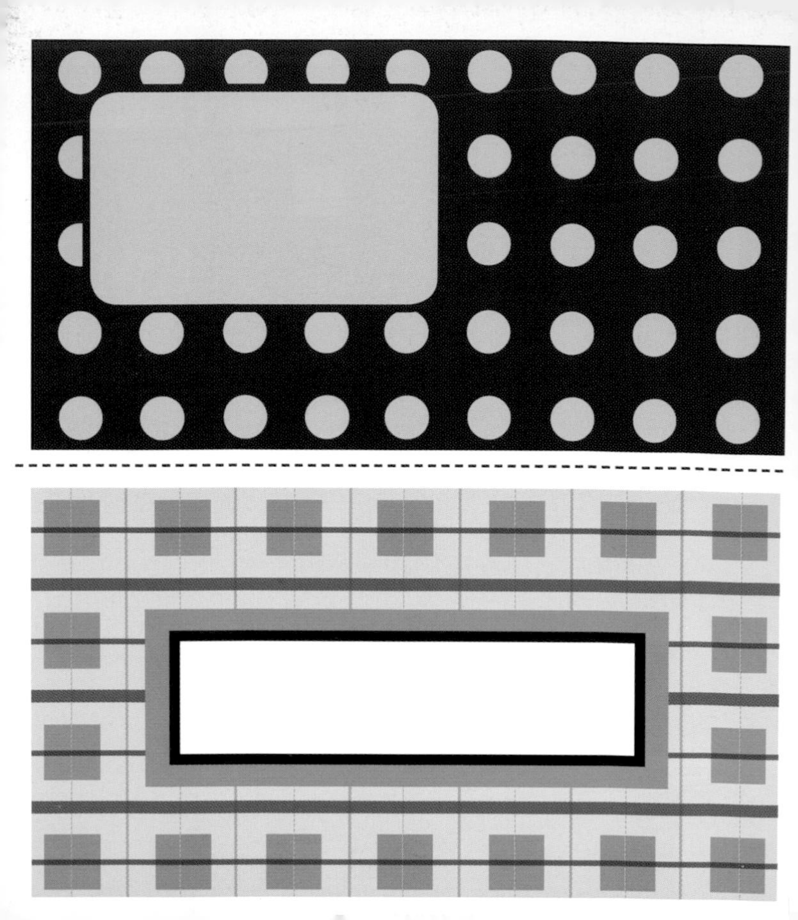

Apple Walnut Cake Mix

¾ C. finely chopped walnuts
½ C. currants
2 C. all-purpose flour
¾ tsp. salt
½ tsp. baking soda
1 tsp. cinnamon
Pinch of nutmeg
1 C. sugar

In a 1-quart container of your choice, layer the above ingredients in order given. Pack each layer into the container before adding the next ingredient.

Securely close container and, if desired, decorate with fabric, ribbon or raffia. Cut out a gift tag with the recipient's directions from the following page. Simply personalize the tag and attach to your container.

Apple Walnut Cake

1 jar Apple Walnut Cake Mix
¾ C. butter, softened
2 eggs
1 tsp. vanilla
2 C. cored, peeled and sliced Granny Smith
or Macintosh apples
Frosting or powdered sugar, optional

Preheat oven to 350°. In a large mixing bowl, pour sugar from top of jar. Add butter and mix at high speed until lightened in texture. Beat in eggs, one at a time. Add vanilla and remaining contents of jar. Mix well and fold in sliced apples. Pour batter into a lightly greased and floured Bundt cake pan. Bake for 50 to 55 minutes. If desired, top with frosting or dust cake with powdered sugar.

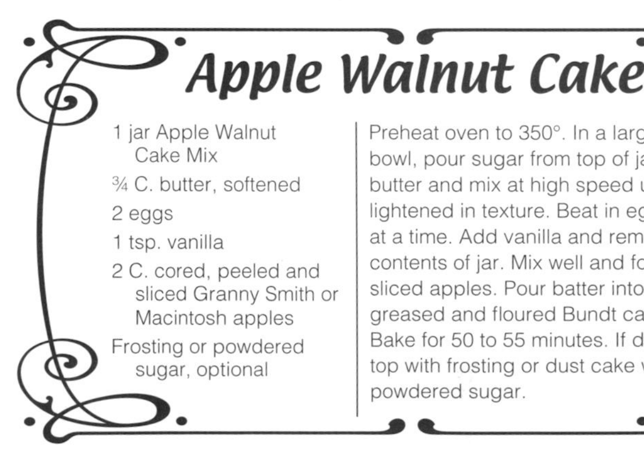

For a quality black and white reproduction, photocopy the above tag. Any of the color tags may also be photocopied for additional gifts.

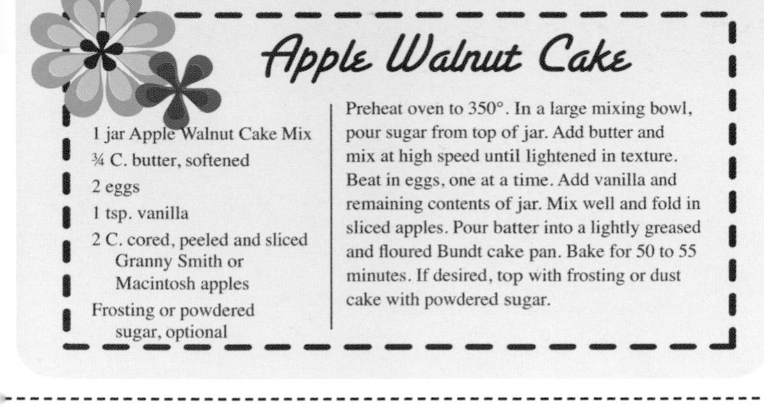

Apple Walnut Cake

- 1 jar Apple Walnut Cake Mix
- ¾ C. butter, softened
- 2 eggs
- 1 tsp. vanilla
- 2 C. cored, peeled and sliced Granny Smith or Macintosh apples
- Frosting or powdered sugar, optional

Preheat oven to 350°. In a large mixing bowl, pour sugar from top of jar. Add butter and mix at high speed until lightened in texture. Beat in eggs, one at a time. Add vanilla and remaining contents of jar. Mix well and fold in sliced apples. Pour batter into a lightly greased and floured Bundt cake pan. Bake for 50 to 55 minutes. If desired, top with frosting or dust cake with powdered sugar.

Apple Walnut Cake

- 1 jar Apple Walnut Cake Mix
- ¾ C. butter, softened
- 2 eggs
- 1 tsp. vanilla
- 2 C. cored, peeled and sliced Granny Smith or Macintosh apples
- Frosting or powdered sugar, optional

Preheat oven to 350°. In a large mixing bowl, pour sugar from top of jar. Add butter and mix at high speed until lightened in texture. Beat in eggs, one at a time. Add vanilla and remaining contents of jar. Mix well and fold in sliced apples. Pour batter into a lightly greased and floured Bundt cake pan. Bake for 50 to 55 minutes. If desired, top with frosting or dust cake with powdered sugar.

Apple Walnut Cake

- 1 jar Apple Walnut Cake Mix
- ¾ C. butter, softened
- 2 eggs
- 1 tsp. vanilla
- 2 C. cored, peeled and sliced Granny Smith or Macintosh apples
- Frosting or powdered sugar, optional

Preheat oven to 350°. In a large mixing bowl, pour sugar from top of jar. Add butter and mix at high speed until lightened in texture. Beat in eggs, one at a time. Add vanilla and remaining contents of jar. Mix well and fold in sliced apples. Pour batter into a lightly greased and floured Bundt cake pan. Bake for 50 to 55 minutes. If desired, top with frosting or dust cake with powdered sugar.

Apple Walnut Cake

- 1 jar Apple Walnut Cake Mix
- ¾ C. butter, softened
- 2 eggs
- 1 tsp. vanilla
- 2 C. cored, peeled and sliced Granny Smith or Macintosh apples
- Frosting or powdered sugar, optional

Preheat oven to 350°. In a large mixing bowl, pour sugar from top of jar. Add butter and mix at high speed until lightened in texture. Beat in eggs, one at a time. Add vanilla and remaining contents of jar. Mix well and fold in sliced apples. Pour batter into a lightly greased and floured Bundt cake pan. Bake for 50 to 55 minutes. If desired, top with frosting or dust cake with powdered sugar.

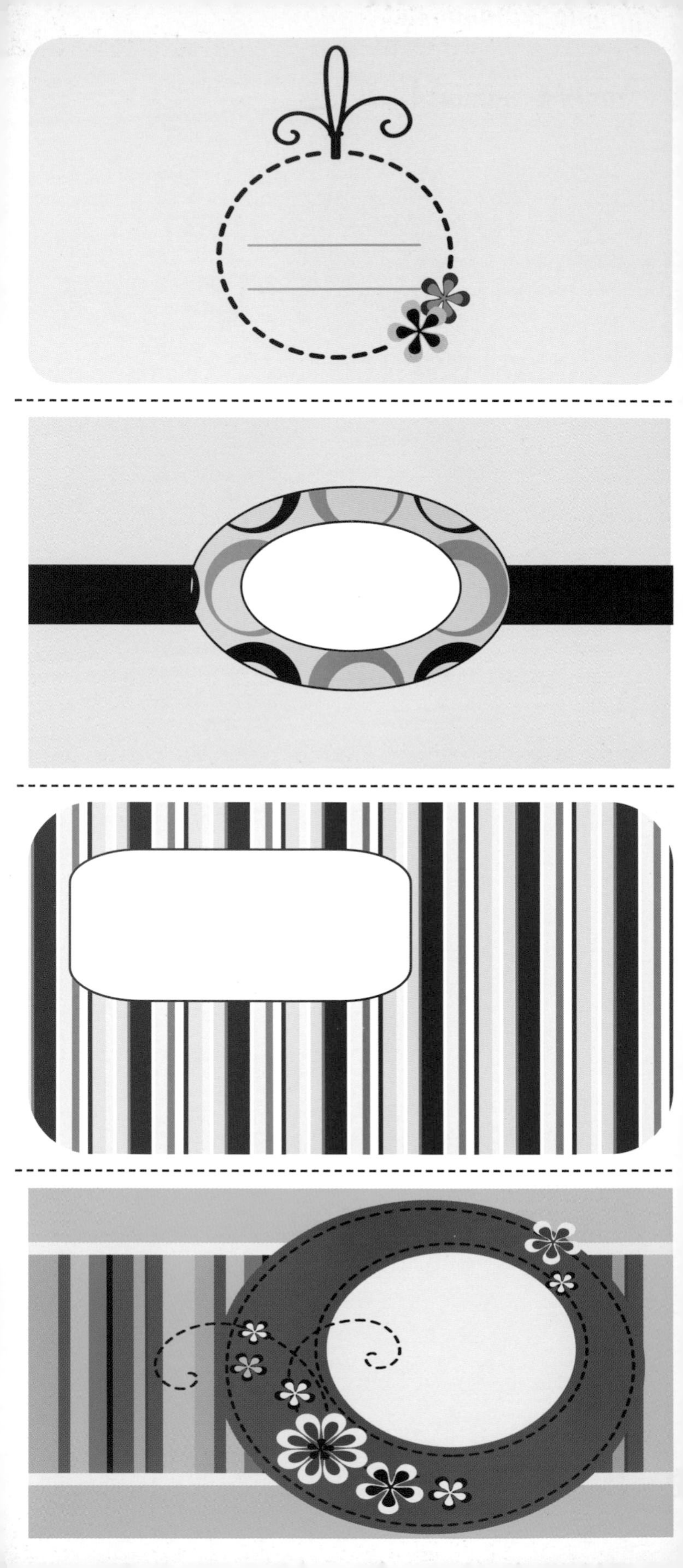

Sugar Coated Nuts Mix

1 C. pecan halves
1 C. walnuts
1 C. cashews

In a plastic bag place:
1 C. sugar
2 tsp. cinnamon
½ tsp. ground cloves
½ tsp. ground ginger
½ tsp. nutmeg

In a 1-quart container of your choice, layer the above ingredients in order given. Pack each layer into the container before adding the next ingredient. Place the plastic bag in the container last on top of the other ingredients.

Securely close container and, if desired, decorate with fabric, ribbon or raffia. Cut out a gift tag with the recipient's directions from the following page. Simply personalize the tag and attach to your container.

Sugar Coated Nuts

1 jar Sugar Coated Nuts Mix
⅓ C. butter, softened
1 tsp. vanilla
2 egg whites

Preheat oven to 350°. Remove plastic bag from jar. In a large mixing bowl, mix butter, vanilla and contents of plastic bag at high speed until lightened in texture. In a separate bowl, beat egg whites into stiff peaks. Fold butter mixture into egg whites. Stir in nuts from jar until evenly coated. Pour coated nuts onto a lightly greased baking sheet. Bake for 20 to 25 minutes, stirring two or three times during baking time.

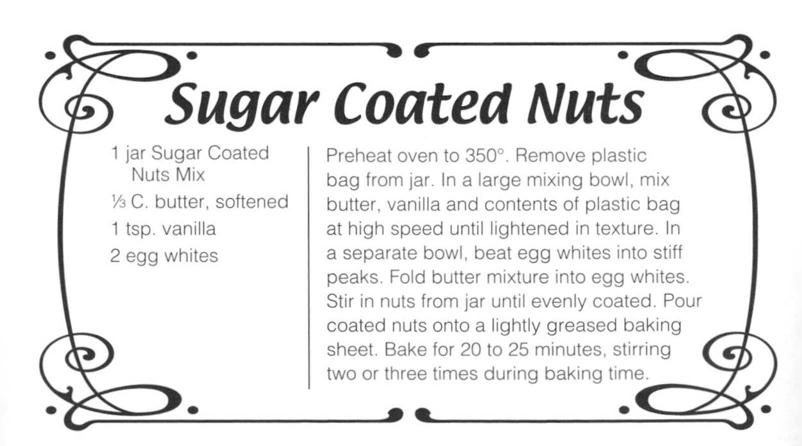

For a quality black and white reproduction, photocopy the above tag. Any of the color tags may also be photocopied for additional gifts.

Sugar Coated Nuts

1 jar Sugar Coated Nuts Mix
⅓ C. butter, softened
1 tsp. vanilla
2 egg whites

Preheat oven to 350°. Remove plastic bag from jar. In a large mixing bowl, mix butter, vanilla and contents of plastic bag at high speed until lightened in texture. In a separate bowl, beat egg whites into stiff peaks. Fold butter mixture into egg whites. Stir in nuts from jar until evenly coated. Pour coated nuts onto a lightly greased baking sheet. Bake for 20 to 25 minutes, stirring two or three times during baking time.

Sugar Coated Nuts

1 jar Sugar Coated Nuts Mix
⅓ C. butter, softened
1 tsp. vanilla
2 egg whites

Preheat oven to 350°. Remove plastic bag from jar. In a large mixing bowl, mix butter, vanilla and contents of plastic bag at high speed until lightened in texture. In a separate bowl, beat egg whites into stiff peaks. Fold butter mixture into egg whites. Stir in nuts from jar until evenly coated. Pour coated nuts onto a lightly greased baking sheet. Bake for 20 to 25 minutes, stirring two or three times during baking time.

Sugar Coated Nuts

1 jar Sugar Coated Nuts Mix
⅓ C. butter, softened
1 tsp. vanilla
2 egg whites

Preheat oven to 350°. Remove plastic bag from jar. In a large mixing bowl, mix butter, vanilla and contents of plastic bag at high speed until lightened in texture. In a separate bowl, beat egg whites into stiff peaks. Fold butter mixture into egg whites. Stir in nuts from jar until evenly coated. Pour coated nuts onto a lightly greased baking sheet. Bake for 20 to 25 minutes, stirring two or three times during baking time.

Sugar Coated Nuts

1 jar Sugar Coated Nuts Mix
⅓ C. butter, softened
1 tsp. vanilla
2 egg whites

Preheat oven to 350°. Remove plastic bag from jar. In a large mixing bowl, mix butter, vanilla and contents of plastic bag at high speed until lightened in texture. In a separate bowl, beat egg whites into stiff peaks. Fold butter mixture into egg whites. Stir in nuts from jar until evenly coated. Pour coated nuts onto a lightly greased baking sheet. Bake for 20 to 25 minutes, stirring two or three times during baking time.

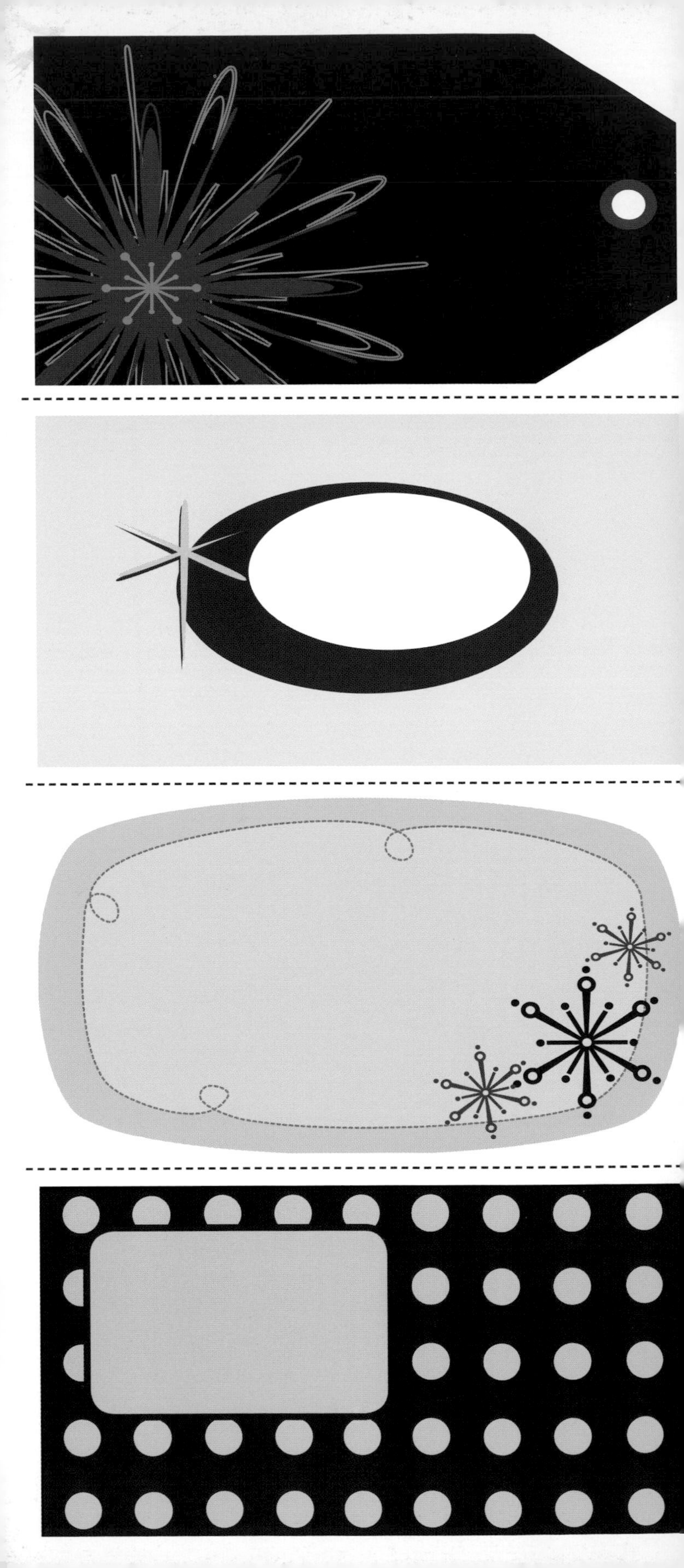

Chocolate-Cherry Bark Candy Mix

1 C. broken pretzel pieces
1¼ C. M&M's
½ C. dried tart cherries

In a plastic bag place:
1½ C. white baking chips

In a 1-quart container of your choice, layer the above ingredients in order given. Pack each layer into the container before adding the next ingredient. Place the plastic bag in the container last on top of other ingredients.

Securely close container and, if desired, decorate with fabric, ribbon or raffia. Cut out a gift tag with the recipient's directions from the following page. Simply personalize the tag and attach to your container.

Chocolate-Cherry Bark Candy

1 jar Chocolate-Cherry Bark Candy Mix
1 T. butter

In a microwave-safe bowl, combine white baking chips from plastic bag and butter. Microwave on high until the baking chips and butter are mostly melted. Remove from microwave and stir until smooth. Allow to cool slightly. In a large bowl, add remaining contents of jar. Pour melted white baking chips over ingredients in bowl and stir until evenly coated. Spread mixture onto waxed paper and chill in refrigerator until set. Break into pieces and serve.

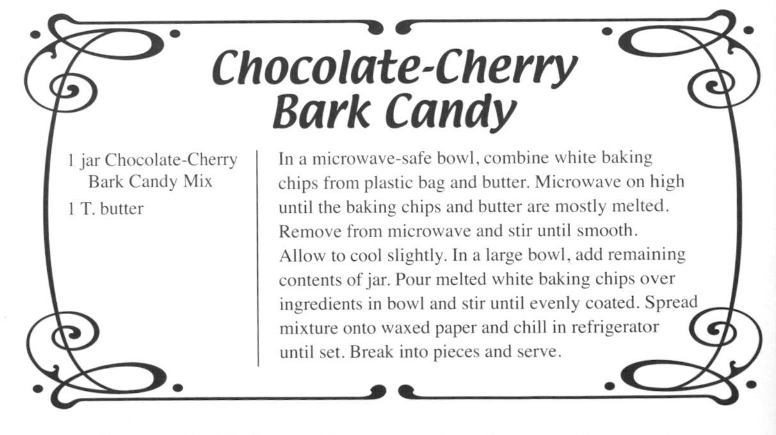
Chocolate-Cherry Bark Candy

1 jar Chocolate-Cherry Bark Candy Mix
1 T. butter

In a microwave-safe bowl, combine white baking chips from plastic bag and butter. Microwave on high until the baking chips and butter are mostly melted. Remove from microwave and stir until smooth. Allow to cool slightly. In a large bowl, add remaining contents of jar. Pour melted white baking chips over ingredients in bowl and stir until evenly coated. Spread mixture onto waxed paper and chill in refrigerator until set. Break into pieces and serve.

For a quality black and white reproduction, photocopy the above tag. Any of the color tags may also be photocopied for additional gifts.

Chocolate-Cherry Bark Candy

1 jar Chocolate-Cherry Bark Candy Mix
1 T. butter

In a microwave-safe bowl, combine white baking chips from plastic bag and butter. Microwave on high until the baking chips and butter are mostly melted. Remove from microwave and stir until smooth. Allow to cool slightly. In a large bowl, add remaining contents of jar. Pour melted white baking chips over ingredients in bowl and stir until evenly coated. Spread mixture onto waxed paper and chill in refrigerator until set. Break into pieces and serve.

Chocolate-Cherry Bark Candy

1 jar Chocolate-Cherry Bark Candy Mix
1 T. butter

In a microwave-safe bowl, combine white baking chips from plastic bag and butter. Microwave on high until the baking chips and butter are mostly melted. Remove from microwave and stir until smooth. Allow to cool slightly. In a large bowl, add remaining contents of jar. Pour melted white baking chips over ingredients in bowl and stir until evenly coated. Spread mixture onto waxed paper and chill in refrigerator until set. Break into pieces and serve.

Chocolate-Cherry Bark Candy

1 jar Chocolate-Cherry Bark Candy Mix
1 T. butter

In a microwave-safe bowl, combine white baking chips from plastic bag and butter. Microwave on high until the baking chips and butter are mostly melted. Remove from microwave and stir until smooth. Allow to cool slightly. In a large bowl, add remaining contents of jar. Pour melted white baking chips over ingredients in bowl and stir until evenly coated. Spread mixture onto waxed paper and chill in refrigerator until set. Break into pieces and serve.

Chocolate-Cherry Bark Candy

1 jar Chocolate-Cherry Bark Candy Mix
1 T. butter

In a microwave-safe bowl, combine white baking chips from plastic bag and butter. Microwave on high until the baking chips and butter are mostly melted. Remove from microwave and stir until smooth. Allow to cool slightly. In a large bowl, add remaining contents of jar. Pour melted white baking chips over ingredients in bowl and stir until evenly coated. Spread mixture onto waxed paper and chill in refrigerator until set. Break into pieces and serve.

Index

Coordinate with Holidays!

- Color white sugar or coconut by placing the sugar or coconut along with a few drops of food coloring in a container with a tight lid. Shake vigorously. Adjust with additional food coloring if color is too light. If sugar clumps, use a sifter to separate. Spread on a paper plate or wax paper to dry. Dry completely before adding to jar mix.
- Consider substituting holiday theme M&M's for regular and substitute dried cherries or cranberries in place of raisins.